THE RISE OF
SOCIAL MEDIA

# THE RISE OF
# SOCIAL MEDIA

ODYSSEYS

JIM WHITING

CREATIVE EDUCATION · CREATIVE PAPERBACKS

Published by Creative Education and Creative Paperbacks
P.O. Box 227, Mankato, Minnesota 56002
Creative Education and Creative Paperbacks are imprints of
The Creative Company
www.thecreativecompany.us

Design and production by Blue Design (www.bluedes.com)
Art direction by Rita Marshall

Photographs by Alamy (AKP Photos, Heritage Image Partnership Ltd), Getty
(Daniel Berehulak, Steve Proehl), iStock (aprott, Aunt_Spray), Library of
Congress (Geography and Map Division), Pexels (cottonbro, fauxels, Changhee
Kim, Ron Lach, mikotoraw, Roman Odintsov, Andrea Piacquadio), Unsplash
(Magnus Andersson, Gian Cescon, Robin Worrall), Wikimedia
Commons (Christies, ConnyPalm, MIAben, National Gallery of Art,
National Museum of World Cultures, Anthony Quintano, Ramy
Raoof, Shonnmharen, TapTheForwardAssist, White House News &
Policies, Wikiolo)

Library of Congress Cataloging-in-Publication Data
Names: Whiting, Jim, 1943- author.
Title: The rise of social media / by Jim Whiting.
Description: Mankato, Minnesota : Creative Education/Creative Paperbacks,
    [2023] | Series: Odysseys in recent events | Includes bibliographical
    references and index. | Audience: Ages 12-15 | Audience: Grades 7-9 |
    Summary: "Teens explore the history of the social media boom from a
    journalistic viewpoint to understand the technological advancements that
    led to widespread internet use and the impact social media has on the
    spread of information"-- Provided by publisher.
Identifiers: LCCN 2022015482 (print) | LCCN 2022015483 (ebook) | ISBN
    9781640267145 (library binding) | ISBN 9781682772706 (paperback) | ISBN
    9781640008557 (ebook)
Subjects: LCSH: Social media--History--Juvenile literature. | Online social
    networks--History--Juvenile literature
Classification: LCC HM742 .W543 2023  (print) | LCC HM742  (ebook) | DDC
    302.23/1--dc23/eng/20220411
LC record available at https://lccn.loc.gov/2022015482
LC ebook record available at https://lccn.loc.gov/2022015483

Inventor Samuel F. B. Morse and his version of the telegraph, circa 1850

# CONTENTS

# Introduction

Social media surrounds us. People in virtually every corner of the globe have their own Instagram page. Twitter allows us to let friends know what we are doing in real time or to follow interesting people. TikTok draws us into watching hours of short videos of people dancing, cooking, or doing makeup tutorials. We regularly check our multiple email accounts, too.

**OPPOSITE:** Technology continues to change how we interact with one another, with many people finding it increasingly difficult to log off and simply be in the present moment.

Many of us wouldn't dream of leaving home without a smartphone to stay connected.

tarting in the mid-1990s, internet-based social media began to form an important part of people's lives. Now, more than 20 years later, social media in all of its many manifestations has profoundly changed the ways in which people all around the world interact. This transformation over such a short period of time has come with both benefits and drawbacks. The rise of social media has truly become a turning point in world history.

Smartphones put the world at our fingertips.

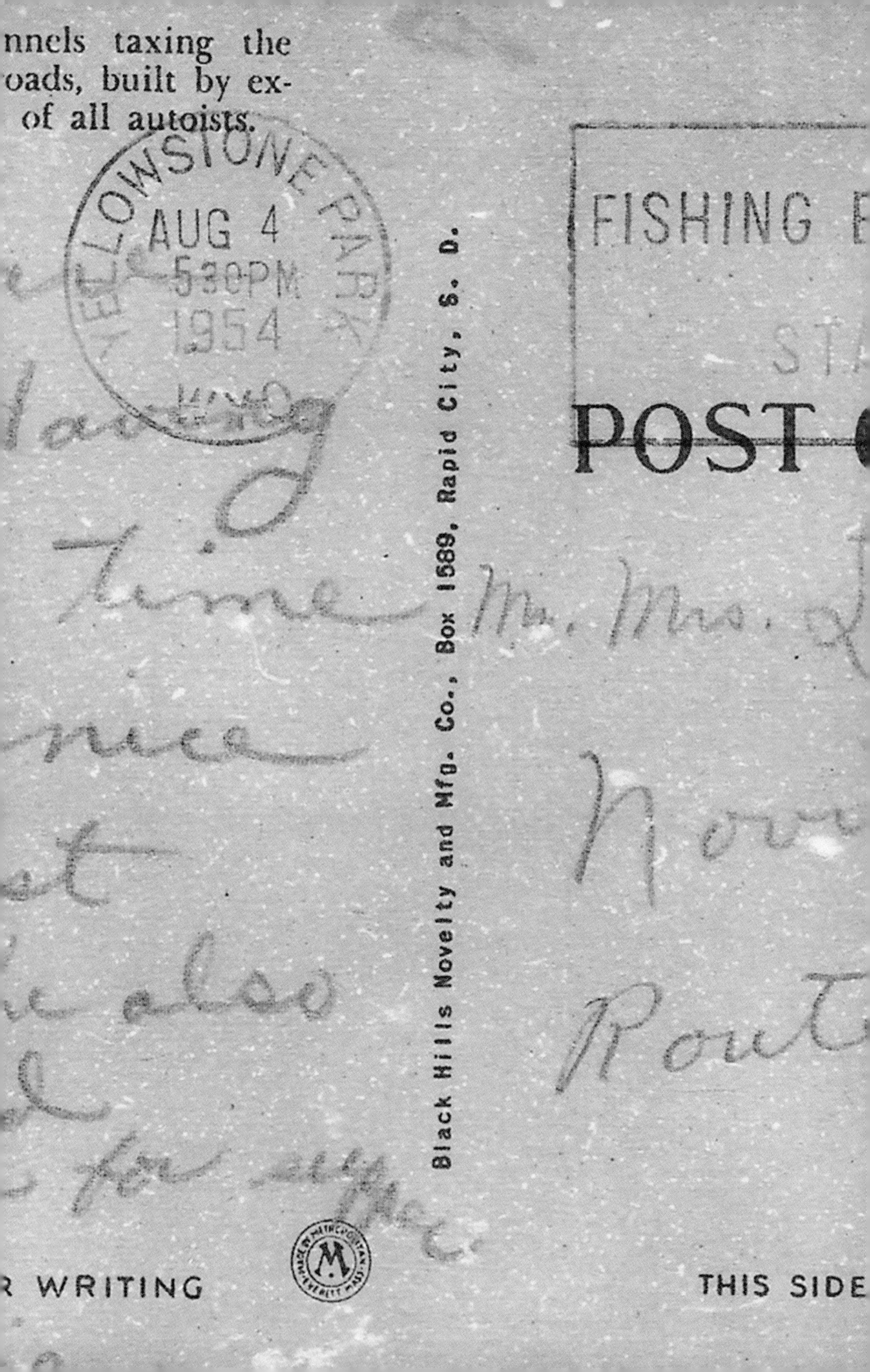

nnels taxing the
oads, built by ex-
of all autoists.

YELLOWSTONE PARK
AUG 4
5 30 PM
1954
WYO

FISHING B

STA

POST

M. Mo.

Nor

Rout

d

Time

nice

t

also

for supe

WRITING

THIS SIDE

# Getting Social

People have always been social creatures. We want to communicate with each other and stay in touch. Many people think that social media began in the latter part of the 20th century. But its roots go back thousands of years. One of the original forms of written communication was the letter. People not only wrote to each other, but they also marked their letters and shared them with others.

**OPPOSITE:** Handwritten postcards once served as social media "posts"—bits of news that could take weeks for delivery through the traditional mail system.

For short distances, letters could be exchanged by people who were on foot. If they had to travel longer distances, letters could be carried by horses or ships. Either way, it was a relatively cumbersome process of communication.

Facebook users today can post messages on a digital "wall," or page. That concept is based on real walls. In Roman times, people wrote notes to each other and posted them on the walls and doors of their homes as well as the homes of others. A church door played a key role in social networking in 1517. German priest Martin Luther was

upset with many of the practices of the Roman Catholic Church. He made a list of those practices he disagreed with in what became known as the 95 Theses. Then he posted them on a church door. They were quickly printed and, as we might say today, "went viral." A friend of Luther's wrote that "hardly fourteen days had passed when these propositions were known throughout Germany and within four weeks almost all of Christendom was familiar with them." Posting and publishing the 95 Theses led to the Protestant Reformation—a landmark event in world history that marked the division of Christianity into Catholics and Protestants.

In the 17th century, another early form of social media emerged with the rise of European coffeehouses. Today's coffee shops attract customers who spend their time hunched over laptops or phones. But early coffeehouses were lively assemblages of people discussing the issues of the day. Many of these discussions centered on politics. In that era, political pamphlets and newspapers enjoyed wide circulation and provided plenty to talk about. The coffeehouses also served as a kind of post office, where people could mail letters or pick them up. In some cases, they even served as commercial centers. The famous insurance company Lloyd's of London got its start in a coffeehouse owned by Edward Lloyd, with a concentration on **maritime** matters.

*The Coffee-house Politicians.*

NCOIS · DVC · DALENCON ·
E · DE · XVIII · ANS · LE · XIX
R · DE · MARS · AN · 1572 ·
S · DE · HENRY · ii · DE · CE ·
M · ROY · DE · FRANCE ·

# Off with His Hand!

An early form of government regulation of social media occurred in
1579. Queen Elizabeth of England was considering a marriage with the
brother of the king of France *(pictured)*. The primary reason was political.
The marriage would unite the two countries against Spain. An English
lawyer named John Stubbs wrote a political pamphlet that opposed
the marriage. After it was published, many people throughout England
read the pamphlet and commented on it. Elizabeth was outraged. She
ordered Stubbs to be arrested. After a quick trial, he was found guilty. His
punishment was having his right hand amputated. It was the one he had
used to write the critique.

Not everyone approved of the coffeehouse culture. In 1673, an anonymous author wrote one of the first criticisms of social media. He called coffeehouses "an exchange, where haberdashers of political small-wares meet, and mutually abuse each other, and the public, with bottomless stories, and headless notions; the rendezvous of idle pamphlets, and persons more idly employed to read them." Still, people continued to gather in coffeehouses and cafes, sharing ideas and building new ones on top of them.

This was the situation well into the 19th century. Whether in coffeehouses or through written correspondence, many social interactions were conducted face-to-face or via personal letters. As is the case today with online communications, parents often tried to exert control over the letters their children sent

"It is anticipated that the whole of the populous parts of the United States will . . . be covered with a net-work like a spider's web."

and received. In one notable case, the future horror writer Edgar Allan Poe had secretly become engaged to a young woman. Her father disapproved of the engagement. So he intercepted Poe's letters and burned them. Because she never received the letters, she felt that Poe no longer cared for her. She soon married another young man.

The invention of a simplified version of the **telegraph** by Samuel F. B. Morse in the 1840s marked a major change in communication methods. Messages were no longer limited to the speed of a ship on the open seas or a person walking or riding a horse. Now they zipped back and forth along telegraph lines. In ideal conditions, they could be delivered to the recipient within a few minutes of being sent. In a short time, much of the United States was linked by telegraph wires. "It is anticipated that the whole of the populous parts of the United States will, within two or three years, be covered with a net-work like a spider's web," wrote one observer in 1848. Messages were transmitted via Morse code, in which letters are represented by combinations of short and long signals (and written as dots and dashes). In an early version of present-day texting, telegraph operators adopted abbreviations to simplify things and speed up transmissions. Thus, "gm" stood for "good morning" and "sfd" was short for "stop for dinner."

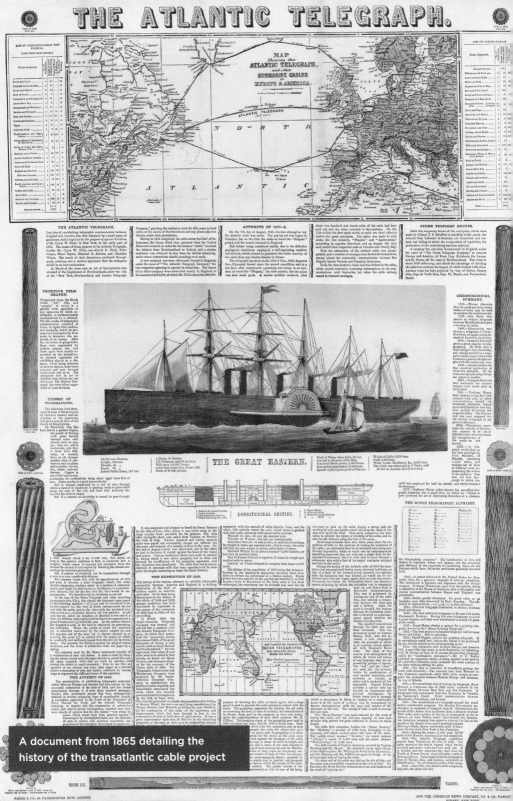

# THE ATLANTIC TELEGRAPH.

MAP showing the ATLANTIC TELEGRAPH and other SUBMARINE CABLES of EUROPE & AMERICA

THE GREAT EASTERN.

LONGITUDINAL SECTION.

THE MORSE TELEGRAPHIC ALPHABET.

A document from 1865 detailing the history of the transatlantic cable project

BACON & CO., 48, PATERNOSTER ROW, LONDON.

AND THE AMERICAN NEWS COMPANY, 119 & 121, NASSAU STREET, NEW YORK.

In 1858, the first **transatlantic** cable was laid. The world was becoming fully wired. Five years later, noted science fiction author Jules Verne—whose subjects included globe-circling submarines and humans landing on the moon long before either of these achievements was a reality—predicted a future in which "phototelegraphy allowed any writing, signature, or illustration to be sent faraway—every house was wired."

Telegraph operators formed their own social networks. During times when they had no messages to send, they

# I Take Thee . . .

In the mid-1840s, a woman fell in love with Mr. B., a man who worked in her father's business in Boston, Massachusetts. Her father disapproved. He sent the man on a voyage to England. Mr. B.'s ship stopped in New York before crossing the Atlantic. The young woman sent him a message: Be at the telegraph office in New York with a **magistrate** at a certain time. He did as the woman directed. She was in the Boston telegraph office. The magistrate performed the wedding vows, which hummed over the telegraph lines. Her father was upset. But the marriage was legally binding. It is perhaps the first example of an "online" marriage.

chatted amongst themselves, told jokes, and even played games such as checkers and chess using the telegraph lines. And sometimes they even fell in love, thanks to 19th-century instant messaging.

The rise of mass communication in the late 1800s and early 1900s changed the social media landscape even further. It began with mass-circulation newspapers, then telephone, radio, and finally television. These new media provided instant communication over long distances. However, only a few people could afford to own them.

And most of the communication was one-way. There was little interaction between media distributors and their recipients.

Yet another technological form arose in the 1930s. Large computing machines sometimes filled entire rooms. World War II (1939–1945) accelerated the development of these machines as warring nations sought technological advantages over their enemies. Computer research continued after the war with the onset of the Cold War, when the U.S. and its allies experienced tense relations with the Soviet Union and its allies. This research took on a special urgency for the U.S. in 1957.

Swedish engineer Conny Palm helped create an early computer called BARK (binary arithmetic relay calculator) in the late 1940s.

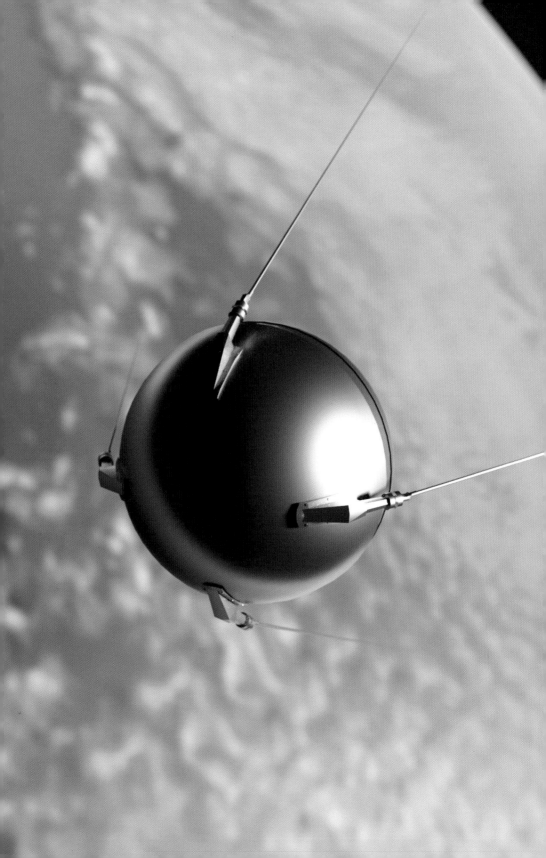

# Networking Media

On October 4, 1957, the Soviet Union launched Sputnik 1 into space. The size of a basketball, it was the first artificial satellite placed into Earth's orbit. Although its scientific value was minimal, it prompted a national outcry in America. The U.S. was lagging behind its adversary in the Cold War. One early response was the formation of the Defense Advanced Research Projects Agency.

**OPPOSITE:** A Sputnik 1 model highlights the famous satellite's metallic shell and four whip-like antennae.

The agency used several massive computers. During the 1960s, the agency's scientists searched for a way to allow those computers to "speak" to one another. The result was the first computer network, ARPANET, established in 1969 to connect four computers. Many more computers were added to ARPANET during the 1970s.

ut as the network grew, it became increasingly difficult for the machines to communicate. Computer scientist Vinton Cerf and his colleague Bob Kahn solved the problem about a decade later. They established the transmission

control protocol (TCP) and then added the internet protocol (IP). Together, these protocols have been described as "the 'handshake' that introduces distant and different computers to each other in a virtual space." As a result, Cerf and Kahn are often called the "fathers of the internet."

By then, one of the most important developments in computer history was underway: the production of lighter-weight and less expensive personal computers. Scaling down the machines made it possible for more people to own them. The three main components—the monitor, the central processing unit, and the keyboard—usually fit easily on a table or desktop.

Personal computers were designed to be easy to operate. That allowed millions of people without a technical background to use them. At first, personal computers were used primarily to play games and complete word-processing tasks. Many new computer owners also dialed into bulletin board systems that allowed them to exchange messages with one another. Companies such as CompuServe and America Online (AOL) offered dial-up services such as email. For many people, email was a huge step forward. It was instantaneous. It allowed people to bypass the long process of writing letters, putting them into envelopes, mailing them, and waiting days or weeks for a response.

Personal computers in the early 1990s typically had a monochrome display and a disc drive for external storage.

# The internet is a global network of computers. The web is a collection of pages.

Eventually, it became possible to access the internet with personal computers. But it was usually a slow process, well beyond the reach of people without specialized computer skills. That was about to change. In 1990, Tim Berners-Lee, a physicist with the European Organization for Nuclear Research, wrote a program called the World Wide Web. The web, as it is often called, is not the same as the internet. The internet is a global network of computers. The web is a collection of pages, all of which begin with the familiar http protocol: http://www. The Google search engine alone contains about 30 to 50 billion indexed pages!

Berners-Lee's original intention was simply to allow his fellow scientists to communicate more easily with each other. Aided by Mosaic—the first browser to simplify internet searches—the web came into widespread, free use in 1993. As Berners-Lee explained, "Originally I wanted it to be the medium by which I could share ideas with people, so it was very much supposed to be a collaborative medium."

The online population exploded. Millions of people created personal web pages that were accessible to anyone. The next step was combining these pages into a network. SixDegrees.com is widely regarded as the first social networking site. The name comes from the phrase "six degrees of separation," a theory that every person on Earth can be linked to anyone else through a chain of six acquaintances between them. The theory was first proposed in the 1920s. It became popular in 1990 with playwright John Guare's play *Six Degrees of Separation* and a film of the same name three years later. A character says, "I find it extremely comforting that we're so close. I also find it like Chinese water torture, that we're so close because you have to find the right six people to make the right connection . . . I am bound, you are bound, to everyone on this planet by a trail of six people."

That seemed like a good omen for a site that was trying to bring people together, regardless of where they lived. When it was launched in 1997, the site included profiles and lists of friends. Visitors to someone's site could click on any of that person's friends. However, it lacked the capability to post pictures. Even though it had more than a million members by 2000, it wasn't commercially successful. It soon shut down. The next social network

# SPANISH
## SHIPS ON
OUR COAST

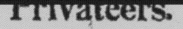

Privateers.

## Fake News

In 2017, the official Collins Dictionary Word of the Year was "fake news." According to the fact-checking website PolitiFact, "Fake news is made-up stuff, masterfully manipulated to look like **credible** journalistic reports that are easily spread online to large audiences willing to believe the fictions and spread the word." Many people believe that Facebook has played a key role in the spread of fake news. Users share stories, believing they are true. In turn, those stories rank higher in search engine results, further increasing their circulation. Both major political parties have claimed that the prevalence of fake news had a major effect on the 2016 U.S. presidential election.

William Patterson.
Daniel McKeown.

# Lighting the Olympic Tweet

Organizers of the Opening Ceremonies of the 2012 London Olympics wanted to emphasize that the digital revolution was as important historically as the 18th-century Industrial Revolution. They gave World Wide Web founder Tim Berners-Lee an important role. The audience saw Berners-Lee live-tweet "This is for everyone." His message zipped around the stadium. "The values and achievements of the Olympics will be amplified by the World Wide Web," he said. "It will be like millions of digital torches carrying the spirit of the Games to every corner of the world. It is an honour to have played a part for such an inspiring and truly international event."

was Friendster, founded in 2002 as a social networking and gaming site. It quickly caught on. Media publicity generated millions of new users. But the system couldn't handle the influx. Pages sometimes took nearly a minute to download. Rather than deal with service issues, its founders devoted their attention to installing new features—which slowed the website even more.

A different approach to social networking came with the launch of LinkedIn in 2003. It was originally intended as a method for jobseekers to post resumes. It soon became a way for professionals to interact with others in their respective fields. It also became useful for recruiters, who could list job openings. It continues to thrive and grow by adding new features. For example, high school students can create LinkedIn profiles to include with their college applications. For security, LinkedIn has adopted the "gated-access approach." Access to someone on the site requires an existing relationship or an "introduction" through one of that person's contacts.

The first big social network, MySpace, was also founded in 2003. MySpace attracted Friendster users who were growing frustrated with its problems. "Users at Friendster could view only the profiles of those on a relatively short chain of acquaintances," according to the *New York Times*. "By contrast, MySpace was

http://www.myspace.co

myspace.

Home    Browse

Chris DeWolfe, Tom Anderson, and other colleagues from the internet marketing company eUniverse cofounded MySpace and sold it for $580 million.

open, and therefore much simpler from a technological standpoint; anybody could look at anyone else's profile." Within three years, it had become the top-rated social network. As its peak, according to *Vanity Fair*, "Each day, 170,000 new members sign up, creating their own pages, filling out profiles, uploading photos, and linking to an extended network of like-minded others. The average MySpace user spends over two hours a month on the site." But MySpace's reign was brief. A social network destined to become far larger and more pervasive was on the horizon.

# Birth of the Giants

The story of Facebook began early in 2004 in a **dormitory** room at Harvard University, in Cambridge, Massachusetts. At that time, many colleges had picture directories of students, which included basic information such as phone numbers. Some referred to these directories as "face books."

Harvard didn't have a face book. Sophomore Mark Zuckerberg was quoted in the school's newspaper as saying, "Everyone's been talking a lot about a universal face book within Harvard. . . . I think it's kind of silly that it would take the University a couple of years to get around to it. I can do it better than they can, and I can do it in a week."

uckerberg hacked into the school's student records. His first creation was Facemash. It showed a series of pages of two students side by side. Viewers judged the attractiveness of the people in the photos. Nearly 500

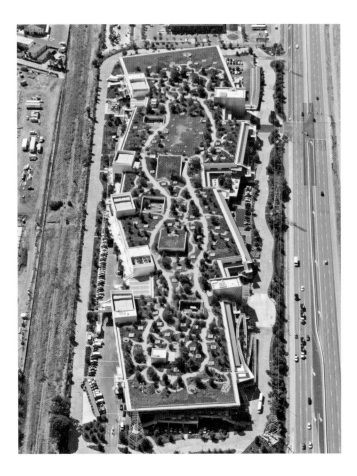

people logged on to Facemash in the next few hours. The school shut it down after two days. That didn't stop Zuckerberg. He set up what he called thefacebook.com. It included a **template** that allowed students to fill in their own information. The site went live on February 4. Within a month, much of Harvard's student population had joined. Other schools quickly showed interest. By May, the site included at least 30 more schools.

Then Zuckerberg traveled to Palo Alto, California. He originally intended to stay for the summer and return to Harvard in the fall. But while in California, he met some venture capitalists. These are people with substantial amounts of money who want to fund **entrepreneurs** with promising ideas.

Zuckerberg attracted a backer. He decided not to go back to Harvard. He was taking the advice of another

noted Harvard dropout: Microsoft cofounder Bill Gates. Zuckerberg once attended a presentation by Gates at Harvard. Gates told his audience to take as much time off from school as they needed to pursue interests that might amount to something.

Armed with his newfound cash, Zuckerberg devoted his time to his fledgling project. He hired engineers and programmers. Early in 2005, Zuckerberg dropped "The" from the company name. Now it was just Facebook. That fall, he opened the site to high school

# The Arab Spring

The Arab Spring began in Tunisia late in 2010 and quickly spread to other Arab countries. It was a revolt against oppressive **regimes**. Social media played a key role in its growth. Protesters created new Facebook pages and used them to coordinate demonstrations. Tweets flooded Twitter and helped demonstrators stay in touch with one another. Unfortunately, the Arab Spring didn't result in an increase in democracy. But it did show the power of social media. According to a University of Washington study, "Our evidence suggests that social media carried a cascade of messages about freedom and democracy across North Africa and the Middle East and helped raise expectations for the success of political uprising."

students. The following year, anyone age 13 or older with a valid email address could join. Membership exploded. In 2008, Facebook overtook MySpace as the top-rated social media site, with an estimated 100 million users. Today, there are almost three billion active users around the world.

Twitter, another giant internet site, launched in 2006. Its cofounders, Jack Dorsey and Evan Williams, realized that status updates would be much more practical if they could be refreshed while members were away from their computers. So, Twitter began operations with mobile phone applications. It benefited from the introduction of the iPhone in 2007 and the Android operating system soon afterward. Those smartphones led to explosive growth for mobile phones using both platforms. Now users could stay in touch as long as they had cell phone reception.

For technical reasons, the total length of each tweet could not exceed 160 characters. Of those, 20 were reserved for the username and routing information. That left 140 characters for the message itself. Users began retweeting and using hashtags. Within six years, Twitter had generated more than 200 million users. In November 2017, Twitter doubled the number of allowable characters, to 280.

Twitter allows users to exchange news and opinions directly with each other rather than relying on outside sources. Author Tom Standage observes that Twitter is more immediate and conversational than other social media outlets. Users can engage in a running commentary on everything from entertainment to world politics.

In 2005, Jawed Karim, Chad Hurley, and Steve Chen created a video-sharing site to make it easier to obtain and share videos. The site became known as YouTube. Their first video, called "Me at the Zoo," was 19 seconds long. Five months later, YouTube had its first one-million-views video. Recognizing its growth and potential, Google purchased YouTube for $1.65 billion in 2006. Today, YouTube has more than two billion users

# YouTube has more than two billion users who watch millions of hours' worth of videos about cats, home improvement, [and] sports highlights.

who watch millions of hours' worth of videos about cats, home improvement, sports highlights, and even **stream** live television.

Instagram was founded in 2010 and rapidly gained recognition. Its name is a combination of *instant camera* and *telegram*—a nod to the first electronic medium. People use hashtags when sharing photos to attract like-minded users. Facebook purchased the social service in 2012. By 2015, more than 40 billion photos had been shared on the site. To stay competitive with other widely used apps, Instagram added new features, such as Stories in 2016 and Reels in 2020, to allow users to record and edit short videos. More than two billion people actively use the app, making it the third most popular social media site.

hort videos have become the preferred entertainment on social media. In 2016, a Chinese tech company called ByteDance created an app called Douyin that allowed users to record videos. Within a year, it had more than 100 million users. Douyin was available only in China and Thailand at the time. In 2017, ByteDance launched an international version called TikTok. They bought

As of 2022, Instagram users in India make up the app's largest audience (about 230 million).

Musical.ly, an app on which people shared short lip-sync videos, and merged the content to create a larger video-sharing community. TikTok grew rapidly. By 2020, the app had more than two billion downloads.

TikTok is one of the fastest-growing social media platforms, becoming more popular than Facebook in 2021, especially among people under 30. "TikTok is so fundamentally different than every other social platform out there right now," said Taylor Lorenz, a reporter for *The*

## Trading Up

Demi Skipper became a social media sensation when she began posting about her Trade Me Project on TikTok in 2020. Starting with a bobby pin, Skipper traded her way up to a two-bedroom house in Clarksville, Tennessee. Over the course of a year and a half and 28 trades, Skipper gained 5 million followers. Some helped connect her with people willing to trade jewelry, electronics, used cars, and other unique items such as a Chipotle Celebrity Card that is good for unlimited free meals for a year. Her last trade included a solar-powered trailer, which she traded for an $80,000 home. In 2022, Skipper gave away the house to someone in need. She traded the house for a bobby pin and started her Trade Me Project all over again.

*New York Times.* The content-geared app is focused more on what people like, not with whom they are connected. Lorenz said, "The primary way that you consume content is through this algorithmically generated feed. You could actually be on TikTok all day and never follow a single person." The app's algorithm curates an endless feed

of videos based on past "liked" videos, comments, and similar videos watched. When many users like and share a video, it can go viral and spark a new trend.

ther popular social media sites include Snapchat, Tumblr, Reddit, and Pinterest. More pop up all the time. A survey in 2021 reported that 72 percent of Americans use social media. Many people belong to multiple sites as the influence of social media becomes increasingly important in everyday life.

Relatively unused until 2012, "selfie" became Oxford Dictionaries' Word of the Year in 2013.

# Pleasures and Perils

In just a short period of time—about 20 years—social media companies have expanded their reach and influence to every corner of the globe. There are many benefits of this expansion. It's easy to connect to someone almost anywhere in the world. You can comment on what they post, and you can read their comments on yours. It can be exciting to post something and see how many people "like" your post.

**OPPOSITE:** Social media allows us to share group experiences, such as concerts and sporting events, from our own personal point of view.

Whether you are in front of your computer or away from home, you and your friends can connect via Twitter or social messaging apps such as Facebook Messenger or Snapchat. Many people have had the pleasant experience of unexpectedly hearing from someone with whom they had lost touch years or even decades earlier.

t's also easier to stay in touch with the wider world. You don't need to wait for formal newscasts or newspaper delivery. Social media has instant information on what's happening, and your friends will provide

## TikTok Made Me Buy It

Influencer marketing is reshaping how brands engage with their customers. There are few sponsored advertisements on TikTok compared to other social media. Instead, brands use influencers to promote their products in an earnest way that seems authentic. Viewers don't feel like they are watching a polished advertisement, but rather they are seeing a real person explain why they like the product in an earnest way. This marketing tactic has been especially helpful to small businesses with niche items. TikTok's algorithm helps promote these videos to similar demographics who might be interested and buy right from the app. This tactic has been so successful that it sparked the hashtag #TikTokMadeMeBuyIt, which has been viewed more than eight billion times.

commentary and links to sites you may not be familiar with.

Businesses love social media. It provides an easy and relatively low-cost way of reaching out to new and existing customers. Many business sites are entirely online and have the capability of precisely targeting their ads to maximize the potential return.

Rioters on the steps of the U.S. Capitol in 2021

**B**ut the rise of social media has had a number of negative effects. "Social media companies have created, allowed, and enabled extremists to move their message from the margins to the mainstream," said Jonathan Greenblatt of the Anti-Defamation League, a group that combats hate speech. "In the past, they couldn't find audiences for their poison. Now, with a click or a post or a tweet, they can spread their ideas with a velocity we've never seen before." Misinformation over the 2020 presidential elections led to an attack on the U.S. Capitol on January 6, 2021. Pro-Trump voters believed the election had been stolen from Donald Trump and were using the hashtag #stopthesteal to spread their message on social media. The ideology spread on Facebook, and protestors used social media platforms to organize their attack. On the day of the riot, a surge of hateful, violent posts and "fake news" circulated on Facebook. Reports of false news that day came in at a rate of nearly 40,000 per hour.

T he sheer volume of daily postings complicates efforts to identify and remove hate speech and deliberate lies. In 2020, Facebook updated their **artificial intelligence** (AI) software to detect 94.7 percent of hate speech that is posted. According to a *Wall Street Journal* investigation in 2021, the technology didn't really work. Facebook senior engineers reported that the company's AI removed only about 5 percent of posts that violated its rules. A 2018 study by researchers at the Massachusetts Institute of Technology showed that Twitter users were 70 percent more likely to retweet untruths than accurate information.

Cyberbullying is one of the most negative aspects of social media. In one survey, more than one-third of middle school students reported that they had been the victims of cyberbullying. Girls are more likely to encounter it. Cyberbullying takes numerous forms. Some of the most common include attacking people online because of their looks, spreading false and malicious rumors, and posting mean-spirited comments intended to be damaging. Others are threats of actual physical violence, hurtful pictures, and pretending to be someone else online. Attacks because of race, religion, or sexual orientation are especially common. The results of cyberbullying can

Although it takes just seconds to post, the psychological effects of cyberbullying can last months or even years.

**OPPOSITE** Limiting screen time, especially for children, on smartphones, tablets, and computers is one way to curb the negative effects of social media.

be severe. Many victims feel a loss of self-esteem, while some turn to self-harming behavior. Even more frightening, a significant number succumb to suicidal thoughts.

Another negative effect prevalent among teens is a link between social media participation—especially on smartphones—and depression. According to a 2018 study, this link coincides with increased use of smartphones among teens during the second decade of the 21st century and helps explain a 50 percent increase in depressive episodes during that time. "The largest change and most pervasive change in teens' lives was more smartphones and more time on social media," according to San Diego State University professor and psychologist Jean Twenge. After seeing posts that trumpet their friends' successes, many teens are prone to thinking that these friends lead "cooler," or more fun,

# There is growing concern about social media's role in mental health and body image.

lives than they do. They may envy those successes and compare themselves unfavorably, thus leading to feelings of depression. "This is not about taking the phone away," Twenge cautions parents. "They are wonderful devices, but it's limited use. Make sure the phone doesn't become an **appendage**."

There is growing concern about social media's role in mental health and body image. Anxiety and depression rates for teenagers have risen in the last decade. More than 36 percent of teens experience persistent feelings of sadness or hopelessness. Social media has made the battle worse. "The **correlational** evidence showing that there is a link between social media use and depression is pretty definitive at this point," said Twenge. "The largest and most well-conducted studies show that teens who spend more time on social media are more likely to be depressed or unhappy."

Young teens are much more vulnerable to Instagram's glamor. The pressure to fit in and look good is amplified when scrolling through pictures and videos of other people's seemingly perfect lives. A 2021 journalistic investigation revealed that Meta, Instagram's parent company, is aware of its negative role on mental health. The company's own research shows that the app is harmful to one in three girls who have body images issues. Some teens develop eating disorders.

What is the solution? To some, it may involve abandoning social media. For most people, though, that is too radical.

Some people have suggested government regulation of Facebook and other tech giants. But regulation can easily turn to censorship. "My hope is that we—meaning both the [social media] industry and all of us—will find a way to keep and improve on what we love precisely by being precise about what must be rejected," says virtual reality and social media expert Jaron Lanier. "The world is changing rapidly under our command, so doing nothing is not an option."

There can be no question that the rise of social media has been a turning point in history. Certainly, it has had far-ranging effects on our daily lives. We can hope that in the future, people will continue to find ways to enhance the benefits of social media while limiting its negative effects.

# Fact or Fiction?

Is something on social media a fact or a hoax? Fact-checking sites such as FactCheck.org, PolitiFact, and Snopes.com can be helpful in deciding. Based in Tacoma, Washington, Snopes is the most popular reference in the U.S. Its CEO, David Mikkelson, employs more than a dozen people to determine what is real and what isn't. Snopes leaped into prominence after the 9/11 attacks. "Conspiracy theories were running rampant," says Mikkelson. "We were the only ones cataloging what was true or not." During the COVID-19 pandemic in 2020, people sought comfort in learning all they could about the unknown virus, leading to a spike in misinformation. Snopes wrote a collection of 18 articles to debunk many of the "infodemic" myths.

---

# Selected Bibliography

Bernstein, William J. *Masters of the Word: How Media Shaped History from the Alphabet to the Internet*. New York City, N.Y.: Grove Press, 2013.

Blossom, John. *Content Nation: Surviving and Thriving as Social Media Changes Our Work, Our Lives, and Our Future*. Indianapolis, Ind.: Wiley, 2009.

Lanier, Jaron. *Ten Arguments for Deleting Your Social Media Accounts Right Now*. New York City, N.Y.: Henry Holt, 2018.

Luttrell, Regina. *Social Media: How to Engage, Share, and Connect*. Lanham, Md.: Rowman & Littlefield, 2015.

O'Connor, Rory. *Friends, Followers, and the Future: How Social Media Are Changing Politics, Threatening Big Brands, and Killing Traditional Media*. San Francisco, Calif.: City Lights Books, 2012.

Standage, Tom. *Writing on the Wall: Social Media—The First 2,000 Years*. New York City, N.Y.: Bloomsbury, 2013.

Turkle, Sherry. *Reclaiming Conversation: The Power of Talk in a Digital Age*. New York City, N.Y.: Penguin, 2015.

Waters, John K. *The Everything Guide to Social Media*. Avon, Mass.: Adams Media, 2010.

# Glossary

**appendage**   something attached to a larger entity; in humans, this refers to arms, legs, or other body parts

**artificial intelligence**
a branch of computer science that deals with the simulation of intelligent behavior in computers

**censorship**   the suppression or prohibition of any parts of books, films, news, etc. that are considered obscene, politically unacceptable, or a threat to security

**correlational**   having to do with the relationship between things that happen or change together

**credible**   believable, convincing

**debunk**   to prove to be false

**dial-up**   using phone lines to establish an internet connection

**dormitory**   a building with bedrooms in a school or other institution

**eating disorder**   a psychological disorder (such as anorexia nervosa or bulimia) that is characterized by abnormal or disturbed eating habits

| | |
|---|---|
| **entrepreneur** | a person who plans and organizes a new business, usually with substantial financial risk |
| **extremist** | a person who believes in using violence or other extreme measures to enforce uncompromising views |
| **fledgling** | something that is just starting out and is not yet fully developed |
| **haberdasher** | a dealer in men's clothing and accessories |
| **magistrate** | a public official who administers the law, which includes the ability to perform marriages |
| **malicious** | wanting to cause harm |
| **maritime** | relating to the seas |
| **regime** | rules of specific governments or leaders, usually oppressive |
| **stream** | to send or receive data, especially video and audio materials, over the internet in a steady, continuous flow |
| **telegraph** | an electrical system for transmitting messages from distance along wire |
| **template** | an overall pattern |
| **transatlantic** | crossing the Atlantic Ocean |

# Websites

**Internet Matters: Social Networks Made for Children**
https://www.internetmatters.org/resources/social-media-
   networks-made-for-kids/
Learn about social networks with demonstrated safety records.

**Livestreaming: Top 10 Tips for Teens**
https://cyberbullying.org/Livestreaming-Top-Ten-Tips-for-
   Teens.pdf
Read these 10 tips on how to keep yourself safe and mindful in
   the videos you share.

**stopbullying.gov: What Is Cyberbullying**
https://www.stopbullying.gov/cyberbullying/what-is-it
Learn about cyberbullying and how to prevent it.

# Index